Abie Longstaff

Letizia Rizzo

Collins

CONTENTS

MAP OF THE REALM 2

CHAPTER 1 4

CHAPTER 2 14

CHAPTER 3 23

CHAPTER 4 32

CHAPTER 5 41

CHAPTER 6 50

BLAISE'S DRAWBRIDGE 60

BLAISE'S NEXT JOB 62

DRAGONS 64

BLACKSMITHS IN HISTORY 66

BLACKSMITHS TODAY 68

ABOUT THE AUTHOR................... 70

ABOUT THE ILLUSTRATOR............. 72

BOOK CHAT........................... 74

CHAPTER 1

Blaise was a blacksmith. Her best friend was a dragon called Flint. Blaise and Flint loved making things from metal! Flint's dragon flame quickly heated the metal until it glowed red.

WHOOSH! went the dragon flame.

BANG! went Blaise's hammer as she shaped the metal.

"We can make anything, Flint," said Blaise. "As long as we're together."

Flint puffed a smiley face with his dragon smoke.

Blaise and Flint practised their craft every day because they wanted to be as skilful as their hero, the legendary blacksmith Valco.

However, there wasn't much work for blacksmiths in the tiny village where Blaise and Flint lived with Granny. One week, a gate needed mending. Another week, a knife needed sharpening. And the Lord of the Manor had once purchased a fire poker.

Blaise sighed. "At this rate, we'll never be as good as Valco."

One Wednesday in January, Flint swooped down from the sky. He landed BOOM! and dropped a piece of paper.

Blaise gasped. "The Silver Castle! That's the one that Valco helped to build. I've never seen it."

Flint puffed an image of the castle.
"You mean we should go there?"
asked Blaise. "Oh Flint, the Silver Castle
is leagues and leagues away."

Blaise looked around her, at the tree
she'd played on when she was little,
and the schoolhouse where she'd learnt
to read.

"This village is all I've ever known,"
said Blaise. "We'd have to leave Granny!"

That night, there was a huge storm.
The rain pelted the roof of their little
cottage and the wind howled.

Blaise tossed and turned on her
straw bed.

Her head was filled with images of the Silver Castle.

"I don't know anyone at the castle," she said, as the thunder boomed. Flint puffed a hand emoji. "I know you, Flint."

Lightning flashed off the shiny metal pots and pans Blaise had made for Granny.

Blaise pictured the fair. "There will be rides and jugglers and games, Flint." She wriggled onto her side.
"And everybody will be showing off their craft skills." Flint nodded.

Blaise nibbled her thumbnail. "If we show our blacksmithing," she said thoughtfully, "someone might ask us to make something amazing. Better than a poker. And Granny could come and visit. She'd be so proud of us!" Blaise sprang up.

"Let's go to the Silver Castle!" she cried, throwing her things into a bag. "As long as we have each other, we can do anything."

Dawn broke on Thursday morning, clear and bright. The storm had passed. Blaise kissed Granny farewell. She clambered up onto Flint's back and they soared away, towards the Silver Castle!

WHOOSH!

Flint glided through the sky, for leagues and leagues until …

"There!" cried Blaise and pointed ahead. "It's the Silver Castle! That's where the fair is going to be on Saturday!"

CHAPTER 2

The Silver Castle shimmered in the dusky light.

"Oh!" sighed Blaise. "It's even more beautiful than I imagined!"

Flint flew closer. He hovered so that Blaise could inspect every silver decoration Valco had made.

Blaise leaned her head on Flint's neck. "I'm so happy, Flint! We'll find lots of work, and best of all, we'll be doing it together."

They landed just in front of the moat. The drawbridge was down, but some of its wooden planks were broken, leaving big gaps to step over.

"I'm not walking on that bridge, Flint," said Blaise. "It's far too rickety. Look!" Blaise pointed up. "There's a metal chain missing. I wonder …"

There was a sound of shuffling footsteps. Blaise shrank back behind a bush and pulled Flint with her.

An elderly guard appeared. He shook his head. "Oh, that storm!" he mumbled to himself, shaking his fist at the sky. "It's done so much damage! Now nobody can get across the moat into the castle. How will they visit the fair?"

Flint nudged Blaise forward with his head. "Stop pushing me, Flint," said Blaise. "I can't just start talking to that guard. I don't even know him."

The guard headed back into the castle.

Flint puffed an image of a chain.

"I WILL speak to him about the chain, I promise," said Blaise. "Soon."
She looked down. She was always fine talking to Flint, and to Granny. But new people were scary.

"Come on," she said. "It's getting late. Let's find a place to put up our tent."

In a nearby valley was an encampment, with lots of people waiting to set up stalls at the fair. There was a jeweller, a candle maker and a leatherworker. As Flint flew by, everyone cheered to see a dragon! Blaise held onto Flint tightly. He was *her* dragon.

"There's a space!" cried Blaise from Flint's back.

THUD! Flint landed on a flat area of grass next to a tent.

A boy popped out from the tent.
"Hello! I'm Ivan," he said. "Can I pat the dragon?"

Blaise nodded. "His name is Flint," she said, "and I'm Blaise."

Ivan stroked Flint's neck. Flint closed his eyes and snorted happily.

"I've never seen a dragon," said Ivan. "But I have Toothy. Toothy?" As he called, a beaver trotted out from the tent. "She helps me with all my carpentry."

Flint bent down and rubbed noses with Toothy.

"We've been busy fixing everyone's tent pegs," said Ivan. "There was a terrible storm last night, and it blew everything down. Oh!" he cried. "Bring Flint to the campfire! It would cheer us all up."

"I don't know –" began Blaise. Flint was *her* friend.

"Please!" said Ivan. "There's a big group of us. You can meet everyone."

A big group? Blaise froze. All those new people! She hugged her arms to her chest. She only needed Flint.

"We'll just make our own dinner tonight," she said.

CHAPTER 3

Ivan and Toothy headed to the campfire and Blaise set up her tent. She made a pile of sticks and Flint blew a tiny burst of flame to light it.

"Can you get water?" Blaise held out a pail. Flint seized the handle in his mouth and flew off to find some.

Blaise sat by her little fire. The camp was filled with the noise of people laughing and singing. Everyone already knew everyone. At least she had Flint.

The flames flickered. Where was Flint? He was taking ages getting water! A happy dragon snort rang out from the other side of the camp. Was Flint with Ivan at the campfire? Blaise twisted the cord of her tunic nervously.

Suddenly, there he was, flapping to Blaise with the pail in his mouth.

"Flint!" cried Blaise. "Where were you?"

He put down the pail and puffed two shapes with his dragon smoke.

"Two pails?" asked Blaise. "Were you getting water for Ivan too?"

Flint nodded. Blaise breathed out in relief.

Flint puffed a picture of the castle.

"Yes," said Blaise. "Tomorrow I'll speak to that guard about the metal chain. I promise."

She tightened her fists. She could do it. She *would* do it, because if they wanted to be as good as Valco, they needed proper blacksmithing jobs.

Early on Friday morning, Blaise and Flint flew to the castle. They landed by the moat again, and Flint poked Blaise towards the drawbridge with the tip of his wing.

"Ok," said Blaise. Her hands shook and her legs wobbled. She stood at the edge of the broken drawbridge.

"H-hello?" she said quietly. Flint snorted. Blaise gave him a look and tried again, louder this time: "Hello?"

The elderly guard appeared. "Can I help you?" he spluttered.

"Um," said Blaise.

Flint pushed his head in Blaise's back. His weight was strong and warm against her.

"I'm a blacksmith," said Blaise. "I can fix your drawbridge. I'll make you two new chains to hold it up."

"The fair is tomorrow morning! You'll never get it done." The guard shook his head. "We'll have to cancel."

Blaise had to be brave!

"If you're going to cancel, you might as well let me try," she said.

The guard thought a moment.

"You have until sunset tonight," he said. "If you get it right, you'll receive a bag of gold from the king as a reward." And with that, he marched off.

Blaise took her blacksmithing tools from her bag and heaved the small anvil down from Flint's saddlebag.

WHOOSH! went Flint's dragon flame.

BANG! went Blaise's hammer.

She twisted lumps of metal into little oval links. She made link after link, until she had long metal chains.

Blaise and Flint fitted the new chains to the drawbridge. They looked so shiny and smart!

"We did it!" Blaise grinned. She was a real blacksmith now! Just like Valco.

She packed up her things. "We need to call the guard to check it."

She turned to Flint, but Flint had vanished.

CHAPTER 4

"Flint?" Blaise called.

A dragon snort came from round the castle corner. Blaise followed the noise to find Flint staring at the moat water.

When he saw Blaise, Flint jumped in excitement and puffed a double heart emoji.

"A new friend?" said Blaise. "What new friend?" Her face grew hot. "You don't need new friends, Flint. You've got me."

Blaise stomped back to the drawbridge. Flint followed her a few moments later.

"Guard?" Blaise called. The old guard appeared. He looked up at the chains.

"Nice new chains," he said. "But the planks on the drawbridge are still broken."

"Oh," said Blaise. "I only know about metal."

"You said you'd fix the bridge!" said the guard angrily. "I want it mended by sunset."

He shuffled off in a sulk.

Blaise crouched down. "We can fix the drawbridge, Flint. I'm sure we can. We just need to fill in the gaps."

Flint puffed a question mark.

"I don't know how to cut wood either," said Blaise. She pulled at a section of plank and it came right out! Her chest was tight. How would she get this mended by sunset?

Flint headed towards the castle corner.

"Where are you going?" asked Blaise.

Flint puffed a double heart emoji.

"No!" snapped Blaise. "You are not allowed to go to your new friend. You have to stay with ME." She was so cross, she dropped the plank in the river and it floated away!

"Oh no!" cried Blaise. "Now there's an even bigger gap!"

Flint puffed another double heart emoji.

"NO!" shouted Blaise. "You are supposed to be MY friend."

Flint started to puff but Blaise was too cross to listen.

"You made me drop that plank, Flint!" yelled Blaise furiously. "This is all *your* fault!"

Blaise stormed down the hill and she didn't stop until she reached the encampment. She flung herself inside her tent and sobbed in anguish.

"I should never have come here!" she cried. She missed her home village, where everything was easy, and everyone was a friend.

She cried until she had no more
tears left. Then she blew her nose hard
and dried her eyes. There was a heavy
lump in her tummy. She felt terrible for
shouting at Flint. It wasn't his fault,
not really.

From outside came the sound of sawing.

Wish woosh wish woosh

Blaise sat up. Ivan was a carpenter.
He knew about wooden planks!
But ... but ... she'd have to talk to him
to persuade him. And Flint wasn't here
to help her.

She poked her head out of her tent. Ivan was by his tent, cutting a long piece of wood.

Blaise shrank back. He looked busy. She could try another time.

Two little girls skipped by arm in arm.

"One more sleep till the fair!" they sang. "One more sleep till the fair!"

Blaise swallowed hard. If she didn't fix that bridge today, the fair would be cancelled!

CHAPTER 5

Blaise took a deep breath.

Before she could change her mind, she rushed over to Ivan. "Can you help me?" she blurted out.

Blaise told Ivan all about the drawbridge and the chains and the planks.

"Of course I'll help you," said Ivan. "I know how to fix a few wooden planks!" He packed up his tools.

"Thank you!" said Blaise. All at once, she felt lighter.

Just then, Flint landed. BOOM!

He nuzzled his head into Blaise's shoulder and puffed a heart emoji.

"I'm sorry, Flint," said Blaise. She leaned her head on his snout. "It wasn't your fault. It was mine. You are right. We do need other friends too."

He opened a wing and Blaise and Ivan climbed onto his back.

"To the castle!" cried Blaise.

They landed at the moat, right by the broken drawbridge. The middle plank was still missing. It had floated away somewhere.

"I've got some wood here to patch up the gaps," said Ivan, "but we do need that missing piece."

Blaise stared into the water. Where had it disappeared to?

Flint puffed a double heart emoji.

"Friend?" said Blaise. "What friend?"

Flint stuck his head into the moat water and did a bubbly roar.

Moments later, Toothy the beaver swam up! She lifted her snout out of the moat water and gave Flint a little kiss.

"Hi Toothy!" said Ivan. He rolled his eyes and laughed. "She's always swimming off to meet new friends," he said.

"Was it Toothy you were playing with earlier?" Blaise asked Flint, and Flint nodded.

Flint turned to Toothy and puffed an image of the plank. Toothy nodded and swam off. Soon she was back, dragging the missing plank through the water with her mouth.

"Hooray!" cried Blaise. "You found it! Thank you, Toothy!" She bent down to stroke the beaver's thick fur. Flint snorted happily.

Blaise leaned against his solid warmth. "Thank you for asking Toothy for help, Flint." She clapped her hands. "Now let's get to work!"

Ivan set up his work table. He showed Blaise how he sawed the wood, back and forth. "I'm making small pieces to patch the gaps," he said.

Toothy caught the sawn-off chunks in her mouth and put them into a neat pile.

"Do you want a go with the saw, Blaise?" asked Ivan.

"Yes please!" Suddenly, she wanted to try everything new.

Blaise lifted the saw and set the spiky teeth against the wood.

"Look at me, Flint! I'm sawing!"

Flint puffed a smiley face.

"Now I need nails," said Ivan, hunting through his tool bag.

"I can make nails!" said Blaise.

WHOOSH! went the dragon flame.

BANG! went Blaise's hammer.

She turned and shaped the metal into little nails.

"Wow!" said Ivan. "That's so clever. Show me!"

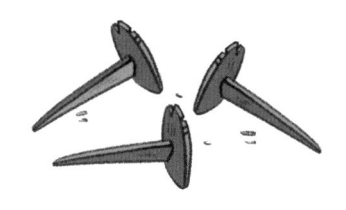

CHAPTER 6

Blaise, Flint, Ivan and Toothy worked hard all day long. Ivan and Toothy sawed little pieces of wood to fit into the gaps, and Blaise hammered them in tight with her very own nails.

Then they replaced the missing plank and fitted it firmly in place. By sunset, they were all finished.

"What's all this?" came a curious voice. It was the guard.

Blaise grinned at him. "We have fixed your bridge." She spread her arms wide.

"So you did!" The old guard nodded his head admiringly at the strong bridge. Then he looked at Blaise. "You're just as good as Valco," he said.

Blaise gasped; "You knew Valco?"

"I did," said the old guard. "He worked with a team, just like you. He worked with stonemasons and carpenters and weavers to make this castle."

Blaise linked arms with Ivan.
"We're a team! And we're much stronger when we work together," she said, and Ivan smiled at her.

The guard handed Blaise a small leather bag.

"One bag of gold," he said. "The king's been asking for a new balcony. I think I know just the blacksmith to make the railings!"

"Thank you," said Blaise.

They waved to the guard and walked off down the hill.

"It will be fun at the fair tomorrow," said Blaise. "After all, we now have a bag of gold to spend!"

"Hooray!" cried Ivan.

Blaise stopped just outside the encampment. "But first," she said, "can you introduce me to all your friends at the campfire tonight?"

"Of course!" said Ivan.

Flint puffed a picture of a marshmallow.

"Don't worry," replied Ivan. "There will be plenty of those."

And there were!

That night, Blaise cooked vegetarian sausages on the fire and met everyone in the camp.

Flint gave rides to all the children and they squealed in delight as he soared and swooped through the air.

On Saturday morning, all the stallholders from the encampment flocked across the drawbridge and into the castle. They set up their stalls, and soon the fair was ready to begin!

57

Blaise and Flint stopped by the moat.
They gazed at the sturdy bridge
they'd made.

"I can't wait to tell Granny about
all our adventures, Flint," she said.
"But let's not go home too soon."

Flint snorted happily.

"We'll always have each other,"
said Blaise. "Valco may have had
a team of builders, but he didn't have
a dragon like you, Flint."

Blaise hugged Flint's neck. "You can go
and play with Toothy if you like."

Flint puffed a clock.

"Yes, I'll see you later," said Blaise, blowing him a kiss.

She walked over the drawbridge and into the fair, to enjoy the day with all her new friends.

BLAISE'S DRAWBRIDGE

WINCH

PULLEY

PIVOT

CHAIN

CHAINS

A B C

BLAISE'S NEXT JOB

Blaise is going to make a coat of arms for a knight. He'll hang it up where he lives. But first, she needs to ask some questions.

Where do you live?

In a castle by a river.

What do you like to do?

Gardening.

What sports do you like most?

Football and jousting.

And what do you like to eat?

Spicy meatball pasta. Yum!

Do you like this design?

I love it! Thank you.

DRAGONS

Dragons are legendary creatures. They appear in stories from all over the world!

They usually have the power to fly, and to breathe fire, but there are lots of different kinds of dragon.

Some look like snakes.

Long Dragon from Chinese myths

Some have more than one head.

Hydra from Greek myths

Some appear on flags.

Red Dragon from the flag of Wales

Some look like other animals with wings and claws.

Amaru Dragon from Inca myths

BLACKSMITHS IN HISTORY

Blacksmiths played a big role in medieval life. In the 1400s, they often had a shop in the middle of town, where they put shoes on horses. They sold nails and locks and knives and even rings. Blacksmiths were so clever at shaping metal that some people thought they were a little bit magic!

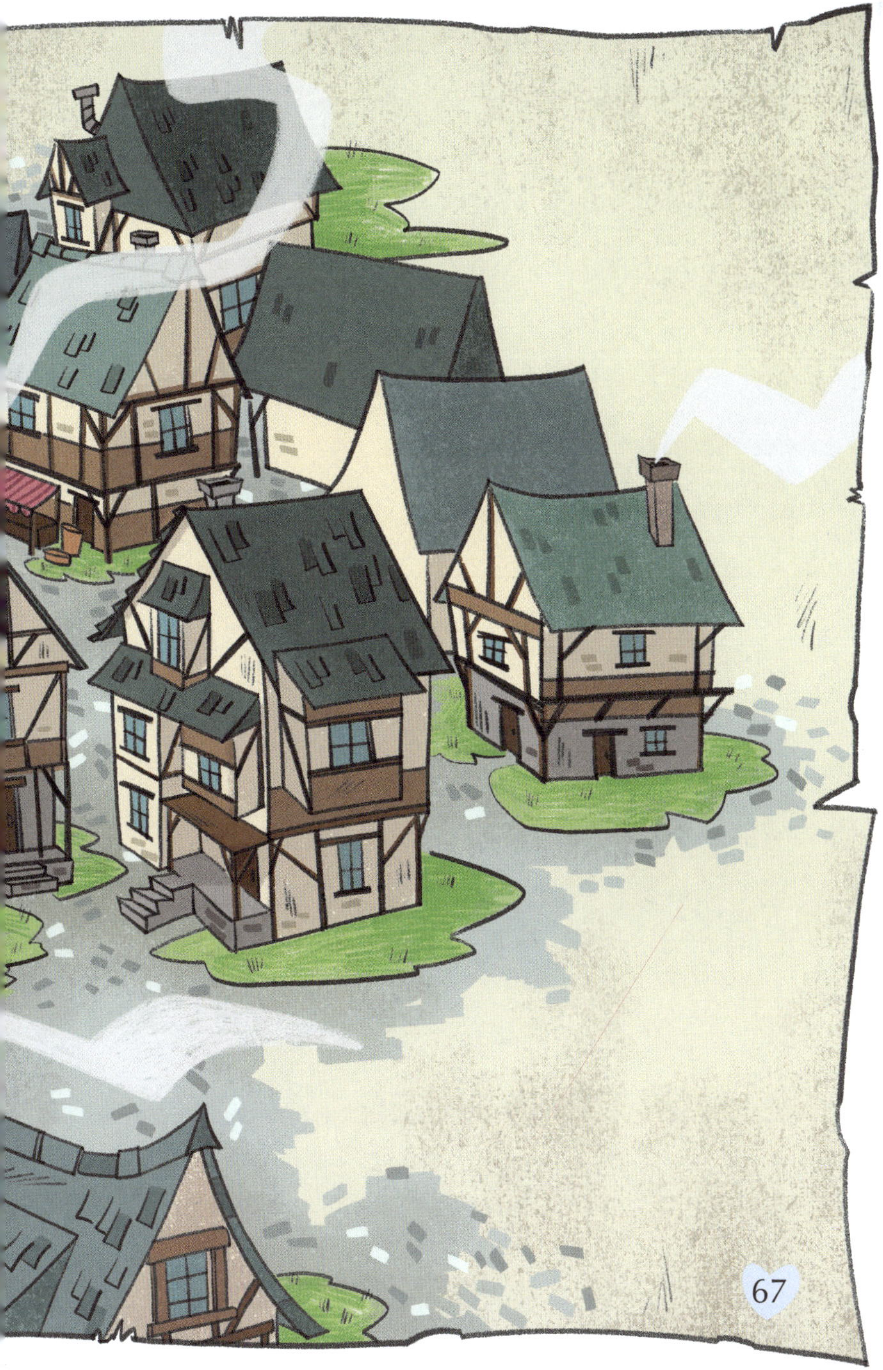

BLACKSMITHS TODAY

Today, you can still find blacksmiths and metalworkers doing all kinds of jobs. But now they also have modern tools to help in their work.

Did you know?

The last name *Smith* comes from an Old English word meaning to hit or strike, and it was used to describe metalworkers and blacksmiths.

Some blacksmiths still put shoes on horses.

Some make household items like curtain poles, balcony railings or shelf brackets.

Some blacksmiths are artists. They make sculptures out of metal.

ABOUT THE AUTHOR

Hi, I'm Abie. I've written over 50 books for children!

How did you get into writing?
I started writing when I was really young, just for fun. I folded up bits of paper and stapled them together to make books.

Abie Longstaff

What do you hope readers will get from the book?
I like how Blaise learnt to be brave. She put herself forward for a job, and she was honest to Ivan about her fears. Sometimes we're so busy pretending to be perfect that we forget that it's okay not to be good at everything. It's always fine to ask for help.

Is there anything in this book that relates to your own experiences?
I grew up in three different countries and went to seven different schools, so I had to learn to be brave enough to talk to new people. At first it wasn't easy and I remember wanting to hide away like Blaise and not talk to anyone.

What book do you remember loving when you were young?

I loved books about magic and portals into fantasy lands. Also, anything mysterious, with hidden doors or puzzles to work out. All those books helped me dream up the kind of stories I write today.

Why this book?

I really like craft jobs — where you make things. I love florists, carpenters, hairdressers and painters and potters. Setting Blaise in a world of medieval life meant I could have a camp where lots of craft workers all lived together making things to help each other. It's fun to all have different skills and combine them to make something amazing!

Are any of the characters based on people you know in real life?

My son works as a blacksmith so he gave me lots of advice about metal. Funnily enough, he didn't know very much about dragons so I had to invent that bit myself!

Which of the characters do you identify with most?

Ivan! He's very positive and cheerful, like me.

What would you make or invent if you were a blacksmith like Blaise?

I love the idea of reshaping metal! I'd probably make lots of amazing sculptures. But can I have Flint to help me, please?

ABOUT THE ILLUSTRATOR

My name's Letizia and I'm an illustrator based in Italy! I have illustrated lots of books. I love reading, drawing, playing the harp, and horse-riding.

What made you want to be an illustrator?

I fell in love with children's books when I was a child. I liked them so much that I started to draw in my exercise books at primary school and on the margins of every essay that I had to write. I think it was then that I decided that I'd become an illustrator when I grew up!

Letizia Rizzo

How did you get into illustration?

After secondary school I went to a comics school and I also attended many visual arts workshops. I got my first illustration job in 2016 thanks to Astound, my agency!

What did you like best about illustrating this book?

Having the opportunity to draw a dragon as one of the main characters was a dream come true! I love dragons and I like to collect books about them!

What was the most difficult thing about illustrating this book?

In this book I had to draw many things I'm not used to, such as the map, the medieval village, Silver Castle and its drawbridge, and so I was a little worried at first. But I had a lot of fun, and I found out that I like to draw these things!

Is there anything in this book that relates to your own experiences?

Like Blaise, I was scared to make new friends when I was younger, and I dreamed of having someone like Flint by my side. But growing up I met so many kind people (and animals) who eventually became my friends, and my life feels richer thanks to them!

How do you bring a character to life in your art?

I usually try to give my characters some features of mine or my friends' ... I think that makes them feel more realistic.

Which character was the most fun to draw?

Flint, for sure! I was a little bit inspired by my dog while drawing him, and this made him even more fun for me!

How did you create Flint – what inspired you?

Aside from my dog, I was inspired by the dragons of my childhood such as Grisù (a little dragon from an old TV show) and Toothless from *How to Train Your Dragon*.

Book chat

Which character did you like best, and why?

If you could have a conversation with one character from the book, who would you pick?

Would you like to read another book that follows on from this one? If so, what might be in it?

Do any characters in the book remind you of someone you know in real life? If so, how?

Which scene stands out most for you? Why?

Do you think Blaise and Ivan will carry on being friends? Why, or why not?

Do you think this book would make a good film? Explain your reasons.

Do you think Blaise changed between the start of the story and the end? If so, how?

Book challenge:
Describe your dream job at Silver Castle and what animal helper you would choose.

Published by Collins
An imprint of HarperCollins*Publishers*

The News Building
1 London Bridge Street
London SE1 9GF
UK

Macken House
39/40 Mayor Street Upper
Dublin 1
D01 C9W8
Ireland

Text © Abie Longstaff 2023
Design and illustrations © HarperCollins*Publishers* Limited 2023

10 9 8 7 6

ISBN 978-0-00-862456-9

All rights reserved. No part of this publication may be reproduced, stored in a retrieval system, or transmitted in any form by any means, electronic, mechanical, photocopying, recording or otherwise, without the prior written permission of the Publisher or a licence permitting restricted copying in the United Kingdom issued by the Copyright Licensing Agency Ltd, 5th Floor, Shackleton House, 4 Battle Bridge Lane, London SE1 2HX.

British Library Cataloguing-in-Publication Data
A catalogue record for this publication is available from the British Library.

Download the teaching notes and word cards to accompany this book at:
http://littlewandle.org.uk/signupfluency/

Get the latest Collins Big Cat news at
collins.co.uk/collinsbigcat

Author: Abie Longstaff
Illustrator: Letizia Rizzo (Astound)
Publisher: Lizzie Catford
Product manager: Caroline Green
Series editor: Charlotte Raby
Commissioning editor: Suzannah Ditchburn
Development editor: Catherine Baker
Project manager: Emily Hooton
Content editor: Daniela Mora Chavarría
Copy editor: Catherine Dakin
Phonics reviewer: Rachel Russ
Proofreader: Gaynor Spry
Cover designer: Sarah Finan
Designer: 2Hoots Publishing Services Ltd
Production controller: Katharine Willard

Collins would like to thank the teachers and children at the following schools who took part in the trialling of Big Cat for Little Wandle Fluency: Burley And Woodhead Church of England Primary School; Chesterton Primary School; Lady Margaret Primary School; Little Sutton Primary School; Parsloes Primary School.

Printed and bound in the UK

MIX
Paper | Supporting responsible forestry
FSC™ C007454

This book contains FSC™ certified paper and other controlled sources to ensure responsible forest management.

For more information visit:
www.harpercollins.co.uk/green

Acknowledgements
The publishers gratefully acknowledge the permission granted to reproduce the copyright material in this book. Every effort has been made to trace copyright holders and to obtain their permission for the use of copyright material. The publishers will gladly receive any information enabling them to rectify any error or omission at the first opportunity.

p68 Parilov/Shutterstock, p69 travellinglight/Alamy Stock Photo